Artists in Their World

Paul Cézanne

Nathaniel Harris

FRANKLIN WATTS
LONDON•SYDNEY

This edition 2005

First published in 2003 by
Franklin Watts, 338 Euston Road
London NW1 3BH

Franklin Watts Australia
Hachette Children's Books
Level 17/207 Kent St
Sydney NSW 2000

© Franklin Watts 2003

Series Editor: Adrian Cole
Series Designer: Mo Choy
Art Director: Jonathan Hair
Picture Researcher: Diana Morris

A CIP catalogue record for this book
is available from the British Library.

ISBN 0 7496 6652 8

Printed in China

Acknowledgements

AKG London: 20bl, 22b, 38t. Photo © 2000 The Art Institute of Chicago. All rights reserved. Mr & Mrs Martin A Ryerson Collection, 1933.1116: 25. Art Institute of Chicago/Bridgeman Art Library: 34t. Baltimore Museum of Art/AKG London: photo Erich Lessing front cover c, 33. A. Bartel/Trip: 27b. Burstein Collection/Corbis: 18t. © Collection Viollet: front cover b, 6t, 12t, 14t, 15b, 16t, 32t. Dornac, Paris/AKG London: 7t. © Harlingue-Viollet: 27t, 30t. Alan Jacobs Gallery, London/Bridgeman Art Library: 28b. © LL-Viollet: 9b. Louvre, Paris/Bridgeman Art Library: 10c. Metropolitan Museum of Art, New York/AKG London: 32b. Metropolitan Museum of Art, New York/Bridgeman Art Library: 14b. Musée du Chateau, Versailles/Visioars/AKG London: 10bl. Musée Granet, Aix-en-Provence/RMN-Arnaudet: 8b. Musée National d'Art Moderne, Paris: 40 © Succession H. Matisse/DACS 2003. Musée d'Orsay, Paris/AKG London: 35b. Musée d'Orsay, Paris/Bridgeman Art Library: 17, 31. Musée d'Orsay, Paris/RMN: 16c; photo Hervé Lewandowski 19,23,29, 41b; photo C.Jean 20c; photo Emile Bernard © ADAGP, Paris and DACS, London 2003. Musée du Petit Palais, Paris/RMN-Bulloz: 36t detail, 37. Museum of Fine Arts, Boston/AKG London: 21. National Gallery, London/Bridgeman Art Library: 15t © ADAGP, Paris and DACS, London 2003, 18b. © ND-Viollet: 26t, 28t. Philadelphia Museum of Art, Pa/Bridgeman Art Library: 39. Phillips Collection, Washington DC/Bridgeman Art Library: 22t. Private Collection, Switzerland/AKG London: 12c. Private Collection/Bridgeman Art Library: 30c. Pushkin Museum, Moscow/Bridgeman Art Library: 41t © Succession Picasso/DACS 2003. RMN-Marise el Garby: 8t. Tate Gallery, London: 13. Toledo Museum of Art, Ohio/AKG London: photo Erich Lessing 35t. A. Tovey/Trip: 26b. Walker Art Gallery, Liverpool/Bridgeman Art Library: 11.

Whilst every attempt has been made to clear copyright should there be any inadvertent omission please apply in the first instance to the publisher regarding rectification.

Contents

Who was Paul Cézanne?

Paul Cézanne is regarded by many as the father of modern art and the greatest of the Post-Impressionist painters. During his lifetime Cézanne contributed to ideas that were to change the way people thought about art in the 20th century. However, Cézanne remained little known during most of his career, preferring to paint in the peace and quiet of the countryside. He was a private man and did not get on well with other people, including his family and friends. Most of the time, he avoided the limelight of Paris. It was only later in Cézanne's life that people began to realise he was the most revolutionary artist of his time.

▲ A scene from Aix-en-Provence, c.1837. Cézanne spent many years painting in his home town and the surrounding countryside.

A BOY FROM PROVENCE

Nothing in Cézanne's early life suggested that he would become a great artist. His father, Louis-Auguste Cézanne, was a self-made man who ran a hat shop in the little southern town of Aix-en-Provence, far from any great cultural centre. He was a shrewd businessman and became wealthy enough to open the only bank in Aix-en-Provence. Elizabeth Aubert, Louis-Auguste's partner, gave birth to Paul Cézanne on 19 January 1839. He was the eldest of their three children. Marie was born in 1841 and Rose was born much later, in 1854.

'... the painter should devote himself [or herself] entirely to the study of nature.'
From a letter written by Cézanne
to Émile Bonnard

▲ The artist's father, Louis-Auguste Cézanne.

SCHOOLDAYS

The increasing wealth of Cézanne's father made it possible for Paul to go to the best school in Aix. He was a good student and became a well-educated man – though later in life, faced with people who made him feel shy, he often pretended to be rough and ignorant.

GOLDEN DAYS

Between the ages of 13 and 19, Cézanne studied in Aix at the Collège Bourbon. There he made two great friends, Emile Zola (1840-1902) and Jean-Baptistin Baille (1841-1918). The boys became a threesome, nicknamed 'the inseparables'.

These friendships were vitally important to Cézanne. He never forgot his adventures with the inseparables in the countryside

▲ Emile Zola, c.1885. Much of our knowledge of Cézanne comes from the letters he exchanged with Zola.

around Aix, especially the summer days spent bathing in the River Arc. His memories and emotions lie behind the many famous bathing scenes he would later paint. His continuing friendship with Zola, who became a leading writer, would also play a significant part in his life.

THE SOUTH

Cézanne's birthplace, Aix-en-Provence, is a town in the South of France, a few kilometres from the Mediterranean coast. It was once the capital of Provence, the south-eastern region of the country, but by the 19th century the town had barely grown and remained a sleepy little place, far smaller than the busy port of Marseilles nearby. The climate and landscape of the South of France made it very different from the North. The hard, brightly lit outlines and strong colours of the landscape may well have inspired Cézanne's painting style, and he returned to paint local sites on numerous occasions. Many other artists were attracted to the South, among them Cézanne's contemporary Vincent van Gogh (1853-90) and 20th-century masters such as Henri Matisse (1869-1954) and Pablo Picasso (1881-1973).

Calais

Paris

FRANCE

Marseilles

Gap

Avignon

Manosque

Nice

PROVENCE-COTE D'AZUR

L'Estaque

Aix-en-Provence

Marseilles

Toulon

Mediterranean Sea

Becoming an artist

Cézanne did not excel in his art classes at the Collège Bourbon. In fact Cézanne and his friends believed he was destined to become a great poet! However, in 1857, he signed up for evening art lessons at the Ecole Gratuite de Dessin (free drawing school). There he learned to draw live models and copy plaster casts of ancient sculptures.

In 1858, Cézanne passed his exams at the Collège Bourbon. He wanted to be an artist, despite doubting his talent – something he would feel throughout his life. His immediate ambition was to study at France's

◀ Paul Cézanne, c.1861.

most famous art school, the Ecole des Beaux-Arts in Paris. But Cézanne's domineering father would not hear of it. He forced Cézanne to start a course in law at Aix University.

COURAGE AND DETERMINATION

In 1860 Cézanne stood up to his father. He refused to register for his final year at law school. Zola wrote frequently to Cézanne from Paris, encouraging him to leave Aix-en-Provence. Eventually, after months of waiting, Cézanne's father agreed to let him go and study in the French capital.

◀ *Dream of the Poet*, c.1858-60, Paul Cézanne.
Cézanne doubted his own artistic ability, but, as this painting demonstrates, by 1860 he had considerable technical skill.

TIMELINE ▶

1839	1848	1852	1857	1861	1862
Paul Cézanne is born on 19 January at Aix-en-Provence.	Revolution in France. Louis-Napoléon Bonaparte becomes president.	Louis-Napoléon becomes emperor of France as Napoleon III.	Cézanne enrols in the free drawing school at Aix-en-Provence.	Cézanne leaves Aix-en-Provence and joins the Académie Suisse in Paris. Meets Camille Pissarro (1830-1903). After five months he returns south.	At his second attempt Cézanne settles in Paris to become a painter.

STUDYING ART IN PARIS

Cézanne finally reached Paris in April 1861. He joined the Académie Suisse, a studio where artists could paint live models for a fee. He made some contacts there, but after he failed to qualify for a place at the Ecole des Beaux-Arts, his doubts flooded back and he could not settle down. Finally, after five months, Cézanne fled home to Aix.

Determined to start a new life, Cézanne went to work in his father's bank. But he was soon doodling in the office ledgers and studying at the free drawing school again. In November 1862, after a year in Aix, he returned to Paris. This time there would be no turning back.

A NEW PARIS

From 1852 to 1870 France was ruled by the Emperor Napoléon III (1808-73). During this period, known as the Second Empire, business and industry flourished. When Cézanne arrived in Paris in April 1861, the city centre was excitingly modern. Baron Georges Haussmann had been placed in charge of a large-scale building programme, which replaced the city's narrow, winding streets with wide, straight roads, known as boulevards. These were lined with trees and large, expensive new houses. Department stores were built and railway lines extended from the city into the countryside to improve transport links. Napoléon created a grand modern capital, and he was so successful that Haussmann's work still gives Paris much of its special character today.

▲ One of Haussmann's tree-lined boulevards in Paris, c.1865.

A violent temperament

Public taste in art during the Second Empire (1852-70) was very traditional. Smoothly painted pictures featured historical events or scenes from ancient myths featuring gods and heroes.

New work was shown annually at the Salon in Paris, but many now-famous painters, including Cézanne, Edouard Manet (1832-83), Claude Monet (1840-1926), and the American James McNeill Whistler (1834-1903), had their work turned down because they painted in original ways. Cézanne's only Salon appearance for many years was at the Salon des Refusés in 1863 – a one-off exhibition held on the orders of Napoléon III – showing works rejected for the official show. Most visitors disliked the exhibition.

▲ Napoléon III and his wife Eugénie. The art world was shocked when Napoléon set up the Salon des Refusés. It was the first exhibition of work rejected by the official Salon.

Cézanne spent most of the 1860s in Paris, with some long breaks in Aix-en-Provence. He soon developed an unusual painting style, laying his colours thickly on the surface of the canvas with a palette knife. The effect is known as 'impasto'. It created an impression of strength and energy, but it was unusual and most people regarded it as laughable. From about 1867, Cézanne began painting strange and violent scenes such as *The Murder* (opposite).

▲ *A Jewish Wedding in Morocco*, 1841, Eugène Delacroix. Cézanne drew inspiration from Delacroix's Romantic figures.

SOURCES OF INSPIRATION

During this period Cézanne may have been influenced by an earlier movement known as Romanticism, and in particular by the French artist Eugène Delacroix (1798-1863). The main influence, however, was Cézanne's own personality. Rude, irritable and suspicious on the outside, but fundamentally shy, he bottled up some very intense feelings which he only released in his work.

TIMELINE ▶

January 1863	May 1863	November 1863	1867	May-December 1868
Cézanne's father visits him in Paris.	Salon des Refusés displays work by artists, including Cézanne, whose work was rejected by the official Salon.	Cézanne gets permission to make copies of paintings in the Louvre.	Cézanne begins to paint strange and violent scenes such as *The Murder*.	Cézanne spends time in Aix painting pictures of the surrounding landscape.

The Murder, c.1868
oil on canvas 65.5 x 80.7 cm Walker Art Gallery, Liverpool

This work is typical of Cézanne's agitated style in the late 1860s. He has removed most of the surrounding detail to dramatise the horrifying scene. The stormy sky, the black earth and the cold grey river in the background focus attention on the actions of the mysterious figures. The face of the killer is hidden behind his raised arm. One of the two women in the picture is holding down the other; both have strange, distorted faces.

'...if you were to interrogate all the painters who find themselves in my position, they would all reply that they disown the Jury [of the Salon] and that they wish to participate in one way or another in an exhibition...'

A letter from Cézanne to the chief of the official art schools of France

Encounter with nature

Cézanne stayed in Aix during the summer of 1868 but returned to Paris in December. There, in 1869, he met 19-year-old Hortense Fiquet. Her calming influence may have been responsible for Cézanne moving away from the violence of *The Murder* (see page 11) towards order and harmony. He returned with Hortense to the South in September 1870, escaping the horror of war (see panel). Here he began to concentrate on landscape painting, an interest that was to last for the rest of his life.

▲ Members of the Paris Commune, May 1871, pulled down this statue of Emperor Napoléon I.

FRANCE'S AGONY

For centuries, France had the strongest army in Europe. In 1870, the French expected an easy victory when the Second Empire went to war with the German state of Prussia. Instead, the war was a disaster. Napoléon III was captured, his regime collapsed, and France became a republic. After a terrible siege, Paris surrendered. Then, while the Prussians were still occupying northern France, the Parisians set up a revolutionary government, the Commune. It defied the republican government, which in May 1871 sent troops against it. The Commune was crushed, leaving parts of Paris in smoking ruins.

During these terrible times, Cézanne, indifferent to politics, worked at L'Estaque in the South of France.

▲ Portrait of Madame Cézanne, c.1875, Paul Cézanne.

PAINTING IN FRONT OF NATURE

Cézanne placed himself in front of nature, painting on the spot. The painting *Avenue of Chestnut Trees at the Jas de Bouffan* (right) features the grand estate bought by Cézanne's father in 1859.

TIMELINE ▶

1869	1870	1871
Cézanne meets Hortense Fiquet in Paris.	France is defeated by Prussia. The Third Republic is founded. Cézanne spends time painting at L'Estaque.	The Paris Commune is destroyed by government forces.

Avenue of Chestnut Trees at the Jas de Bouffan, c.1871

oil on canvas 38.1 x 46 cm Tate Gallery, London

Cézanne's father bought the Jas de Bouffan, which consisted of a large country house, gardens and a pool, in 1859 for the sum of 85,000 francs. Cézanne went there often and seems to have been calmed and liberated by painting landscapes in the open air of the surrounding countryside. This fine early example is quite dark in tone – a style very fashionable at the time. But Cézanne's taste for visible, parallel brush strokes, rather than a smooth finish, can already be clearly seen.

'...all the pictures painted inside, in the studio, will never be as good as those done outside. When out-of-door scenes are represented, the contrasts between the figures and the ground is astounding and the landscape is magnificent.'

From a letter by Cézanne to Emile Zola

The Impressionist revolution

For most of the 19th century the Salon in Paris only exhibited traditional paintings. This type of painting came to be known as 'academic art', because it was taught at the state art academies. The Salon-going public, usually people from the wealthy middle classes, was influenced by the opinion of tutors and critics and they bought academic paintings and sculptures in large quantities.

REBEL ARTISTS

By the 1860s, some painters were striking out in new directions. Even though their works were often laughed at and frequently rejected by the Salon jury as not good enough to be exhibited, they kept trying to work in new ways. The most important of these rebels were the Impressionists. They were not a formal group, committed to painting in exactly the same way, but they were all in rebellion against academic art. They were interested in painting scenes from everyday life with a new freshness that captured an impression of the moment on canvas.

▲ Edouard Manet, c.1860. Manet's paintings of nude women caused a scandal at the Salon during the 1860s.

▲ *The Rehearsal of the Ballet on Stage*, c.1878-79, Edgar Degas. Unlike other Impressionists, Degas painted in his studio rather than working in the open air.

The leading figures in the group in the early 1860s, when Cézanne had just moved to Paris, were Edouard Manet and Edgar Degas (1834-1917). Manet chose subjects from his own time, boldly coloured and outlined, that academic painters mostly ignored. His paintings of nudes looked like real women – not goddesses of mythology – and caused a scandal. Degas was equally modern and original, showing his scenes from racecourses, ballets and cafés.

PAINTING FROM NATURE

Claude Monet, Auguste Renoir (1841-1919), Camille Pissarro (1830-1903) and eventually, Paul Cézanne, developed a new kind of landscape painting. They worked in the open air and painted very rapidly, trying to capture the look of the light before it changed. They used swift touches of pure colour to build up their pictures. This was a completely new way of painting, full of life and movement.

STRUGGLING FOR RECOGNITION

In 1874, when the Impressionists broke away from the Salon and held their own exhibition, many people attacked their efforts. It was at this time that the name 'Impressionist' was first used. An art critic jeered that Monet's painting *Impression: Sunrise* was just an impression – a sketch, not a proper painting. Starting as a term of abuse, the word became accepted as the name of the movement.

The Impressionists held seven more exhibitions between 1876 and 1886, but it took many more years for their works to be recognized. Now Impressionist paintings are probably the most popular of all works of art.

◀ An anti-Impressionist cartoon, 1876. Critics made fun of the Impressionists in many ways. This cartoon shows people running away in horror after seeing their paintings.

Cézanne, Impressionist

▲ Pissarro and Cézanne, c.1873.

For most of 1872-73 Cézanne lived with Hortense and his son Paul in the little village of Auvers, just outside Paris. There he was close to the Impressionist painter Camille Pissarro, whom he met in Paris in 1861. Every day Cézanne tramped to Pissarro's home at Pontoise and the two artists worked side by side in the open air. Cézanne learned Impressionist techniques from Pissarro, even copying paintings by the older artist.

◀ Cézanne's folding paint palette. Cézanne used this palette when painting with Pissarro in the countryside around Pontoise. From the paint that remains, you can see how he blended his colours together so he could apply them quickly to the canvas.

CAMILLE PISSARRO

Pissarro was the oldest of the Impressionists. Born into a Jewish family in the Danish-ruled Virgin Islands (West Indies), he was educated in France, where he settled after travelling in Venezuela, South America. Pissarro was an outstanding painter in his own right and also a fatherly figure with a gift for teaching. He was probably the only artist that the touchy Cézanne would have been prepared to learn from; Cézanne, rarely complimentary, called him 'the humble and colossal Pissarro'. An idealistic socialist, Pissarro painted landscapes and scenes of country life and work. In his old age, nearly blind, he also painted city views from hotel windows.

A RARE SUCCESS

When the first Impressionist Exhibition was held in 1874, three of Cézanne's paintings were shown. One, *The House of the Hanged Man*, was sold – a very rare event for Cézanne. As this painting demonstrates, the light, sketchy forms of Impressionist painting (see pages 14-15) never fully satisfied Cézanne. He favoured more structured compositions and defined forms. This, he believed, would enable him to create a modern equivalent to the great art of the past.

TIMELINE ▶

1872	1873	December 1873	April-May 1874
Cézanne's son Paul is born. Cézanne works with Pissarro at Pontoise.	Cézanne spends the year in Auvers with Hortense and Paul. He works with Pissarro almost every day.	The Impressionists form a co-operative society to organize an exhibition.	Cézanne shows three canvases at the first Impressionist Exhibition in Paris. *The House of the Hanged Man* is purchased at the exhibition.

The House of the Hanged Man, 1873

oil on canvas 55 x 66 cm Musée d'Orsay, Paris

The House of the Hanged Man is considered to be the masterpiece of Cézanne's Impressionist period. The impact of Impressionism on Cézanne, and the influence of Pissarro, are evident in the dramatic change in the overall tones of the painting. They are much brighter than in *Avenue of Chestnut Trees at the Jas de Bouffan* (see page 13). However, the solid forms, built-up through the gradual application of different layers of paint, show that Cézanne was not content simply to copy the Impressionists. He adapted their techniques to create a style entirely his own.

'If you're looking for five-legged sheep, I think Cézanne might be to your liking, for he has studies that are quite strange and seen in a unique way.'

Pissarro talking about Cézanne

Difficult times

◀ *Portrait of Victor Chocquet*, 1877, Paul Cézanne. Chocquet bought his first painting by Cézanne in 1875. The two men became friends through their shared interest in the work of Eugène Delacroix. Chocquet was one of the most influential French art collectors of the nineteenth century.

SELF-PORTRAITS

Portraits tend to be commissioned and then painted. By contrast, self-portraits are more often painted for the private satisfaction of the artist. Sometimes in the 15th and 16th centuries, artists painted themselves into large pictures as members of a crowd. However, the German artist Albrecht Dürer (1471-1528) made his self-portrait an examination of the state of his soul. Then, in the 17th century, the Dutch painter Rembrandt (1606-69) painted a large number of self-portraits that reflected his fortunes and bodily ageing. After this, many great artists were attracted to self-portraiture.

▲ *Self-Portrait at the Age of 63, 1669*, Rembrandt.

The 1870s were difficult for Cézanne. He did not dare tell his father about Hortense and Paul, and kept them hidden away. He could not make a living by painting, so he was dependent on the small allowance that his father gave him. However, in 1875, he found his first proper patron (regular purchaser) in Victor Chocquet (1821-1891), a retired customs officer whose wife had inherited money. Eventually Chocquet bought 36 of Cézanne's paintings.

CAPTURING THE EFFECTS OF TIME

During the 1870s, Cézanne created a number of self-portraits. Like the example opposite, his early self-portraits do not flatter him or show him painting. He portrays himself as balding, burly, unkempt and usually scowling. Here he is posed in front of a landscape by a painter friend, Armand Guillaumin (1841-1927).

TIMELINE ▶

Summer 1874	1875	1876	June-July 1876	1877
Cézanne spends the summer painting in Aix before moving back to Paris.	Cézanne meets Victor Chocquet, his first proper patron.	The second Impressionist Exhibition takes place. Cézanne does not take part. His Salon piece is refused.	Cézanne paints pieces for Chocquet in L'Estaque.	Cézanne shows 16 works at the third Impressionist Exhibition.

Self-Portrait, c.1875

oil on canvas 64 x 53 cm Musée d'Orsay, Paris

Self-Portrait was never intended to be glamorous, but instead captures the effect that recent difficulties have had on the artist. Cézanne gives the painting tremendous impact by applying long, thick strokes of paint which can be clearly seen.

Finding his way

In August 1877, in contrast to his usual behaviour, Cézanne began to socialise. He frequented a café called the Nouvelle-Athènes in Paris and attended dinner parties with Manet and influential writers including Stéphane Mallarmé (1842-98). Cézanne had developed his own unique painting style, and it seemed as though he was becoming more confident.

His portrait of Hortense is strikingly original. Her features, although not detailed, are calm and serene. Cézanne's complementary arrangement of colours ensures every area of the painting has its own strength and solidity – even the wallpaper.

ÉMILE ZOLA

Zola was a year younger than his boyhood friend Cézanne. His father, an Italian engineer, died suddenly, leaving Zola and his mother in poverty. In 1858 Zola was forced to leave his friends in Aix and travel to Paris. After a hard struggle he became a journalist and art critic, championing Manet and other Impressionists. In the 1870s Zola published a series of novels describing almost every aspect of French society, from peasants and mining communities to the world of high finance. These works, which exposed greed and corruption, made Zola famous – and rich.

▲ Émile Zola, c.1890. Zola was not only Cézanne's close friend, but also a collector of his work. He eventually owned 12 paintings by Cézanne.

◀ Interior of the Nouvelle-Athènes, c.1880, Jean-Louis Forain (1852-1931). Many artists, including Degas, frequented this Parisian café.

RETURN TO THE SOUTH

In the spring of 1878, Cézanne decided to leave the capital and return to the South of France to spend time with his family. Shortly after Cézanne's arrival his father discovered the existence of Hortense and Paul, and threatened to cut off his allowance.

Already struggling to survive, Cézanne was forced to ask his friend Zola for money. Later in the year, although he had been angry at first, Cézanne's father relented and actually increased his son's allowance.

TIMELINE ▶

1877	1878	1878	1879
Cézanne, feeling unusually sociable, often sees fellow painters at Parisian cafés and dinner parties.	Cézanne's father discovers, and grudgingly accepts, that his son has a family.	Cézanne paints in the countryside with Adolphe Monticelli (1824-86) whom he met in Paris the previous year.	The fourth Impressionist Exhibition. Once again, Cézanne does not take part.

Madame Cézanne in a Red Armchair, 1877

oil on canvas 72.5 x 56 cm Museum of Fine Arts, Boston, Massachusetts

This is not the artist's attempt at a realistic portrait of his wife, but a balanced patterning of blues, greens and contrasting reds. The setting has been identified as the apartment in Paris where Cézanne was living at the time.

Constructing landscapes

▲ *The Luncheon of the Boating Party*, 1881, Pierre-Auguste Renoir. The light, gentle tones of this painting illustrate the relaxed atmosphere of holiday-makers by the River Seine.

Early in April 1879 Cézanne moved to Melun near Paris. He spent his time here painting local landscapes.

The Bridge at Maincy is an example of his 'constructive brushwork' – visible brushstrokes that are organized into blocks of parallel marks. These create a strong surface pattern and greatly increase the impact of his pictures. However, despite Cézanne's efforts his Salon entries continued to be refused – although he did manage to sneak one portrait into the 1882 exhibition.

> *'I am still trying to find my way as a painter.'*
>
> Paul Cézanne

AROUND PARIS

Maincy, near Melun, was one of many places around Paris that inspired French painters. Artists like Cézanne, Pissarro and Renoir could live cheaply, and find landscapes and other subjects to paint, in places such as Pontoise, Auvers and Melun. At the same time they were close to the capital, with its cafés, studios and Salons.

The development of the railway system brought holiday-makers as well as artists to resorts along the River Seine. Impressionist painters were particularly attracted by the combination of nature, boating and picnics, creating breezy, light-hearted pictures of Bougival, Argenteuil and other riverside spots.

A VISIT FROM RENOIR

Cézanne moved to Pontoise in 1881 and then to L'Estaque in the South. Here he was visited in 1882 by Pierre-Auguste Renoir (1841-1919). They spent a month painting together before Renoir fell ill with pneumonia. Cézanne nursed Renoir through his illness.

▲ Pierre-Auguste Renoir, c.1885.

TIMELINE ▶

1879-80	May 1881	1882	January-February 1882	1882
Cézanne spends a year at Melun, outside Paris.	Cézanne moves with Hortense and Paul to Pontoise where he works with Pissarro.	Cézanne moves to the South of France and spends time in L'Estaque, Aix and Marseilles.	Renoir visits Cézanne at L'Estaque where the two artists work together. Renoir falls ill and is nursed by Cézanne.	One of Cézanne's paintings is accepted for the Salon.

The Bridge at Maincy, 1879-80

oil on canvas 58.5 x 72.5 cm Musée d'Orsay, Paris

This painting displays Cézanne's ability to portray nature and transform it into art. It is not just the patterned surface of the painting that makes this picture exciting, but also the way Cézanne creates a sense of place. He uses lines for the trees and blocks of colour for the stone of the bridge. All the forms in the picture, including the reflections, are solid and linked together.

'[I want]…to make of Impressionism something solid and durable like the art in museums.'

Paul Cézanne

Financial freedom

▲ An illustration from Zola's novel *L'Oeuvre* showing the artist in his studio.

THE MASTERPIECE

In 1886 Zola published a novel, *L'Oeuvre* usually translated as *The Masterpiece*, about a group of artists. It was based almost entirely on his youthful involvement with the Impressionist painters and his friendship with Cézanne. The main character, Claude Lantier, resembles Cézanne in (among other things) his Provençal background, his temper and timidity, and his black moods of self-doubt. However, in the story Lantier finally fails in his artistic ambitions and ends his life in madness and death.

Possibly Zola did not realize how this would hurt his friend. After Cézanne received and read a copy of *L'Oeuvre*, he replied briefly, recalling old times (see page 43). Sadly the friends never spoke to or wrote to each other again.

During the early 1880s Cézanne spent most of his time in his native Provence. Very soon only a few fellow-painters, including Monet and Renoir (who visited Cézanne in the winter of 1883), knew that he was still painting at all!

CHANGING TIMES

In 1886, around the time Cézanne painted *The Bay of Marseilles Seen from L'Estaque*, important changes happened in his life. In April his friendship with Zola came to an abrupt end (see panel). At the same time Cézanne's parents finally approved of his relationship with Hortense. On 28 April the couple were married at the Hôtel de Ville in Aix-en-Provence.

▲ The Jas de Bouffan, c.1860, shortly after it was first occupied by the Cézanne family.

Sadly, in October 1886, Cézanne's 88-year-old father died. As the eldest child Cézanne inherited the Jas de Bouffan and a substantial fortune. From now on he could support his family, travel and paint – free of money worries.

TIMELINE ▶

30 April 1883	Winter 1883	April 1886	October 1886	1887
Manet dies. Cézanne describes his death as a catastrophe.	Cézanne is visited in Provence by Monet and Renoir.	End of Cézanne's friendship with Zola. Cézanne marries Hortense.	Cézanne's father dies at the Jas de Bouffan. Cézanne inherits the family house and has enough money to support his family.	In Paris Cézanne is almost forgotten. Some think that he must be dead.

The Bay of Marseilles Seen from L'Estaque, c.1886

oil on canvas 80.2 x 100.6 cm Art Institute of Chicago, Mr and Mrs Martin A. Ryerson Collection, Chicago

The village and area of L'Estaque, where Cézanne worked many times from the 1860s, appears in the foreground. Cézanne captures the strong southern colours, and balances the natural forms of the sea and the rolling hills with the geometry of the village houses. This is one of Cézanne's finest pictures of the Mediterranean region. Later L'Estaque became a popular artists' resort.

'... climbing the hills as the sun goes down one has a glorious view of Marseilles in the background and the islands...'

Paul Cézanne

Provence

Cézanne was a native of Provence, an area in the South of France with a special character of its own. The region lies in the south-east, between the Alps and the River Rhône. Its southern border is the Mediterranean Sea.

▲ The port of Marseilles, 1890. The city is the oldest in France, dating back some 2,500 years.

LAND OF INSPIRATION

In some ways the natives of Provence, known as Provençals, had more in common with other peoples of the sun-drenched Mediterranean than with their French compatriots further north.

The landscape of Provence, so often captured in Cézanne's paintings, was rugged and intensely coloured. Its mountains and gorges, deep greenery and intensely blue seas and skies made a strong contrast with its cube-like houses with orange roofs. As well as its baking heat, Provence is famous for a cold wind, the *mistral*, that sometimes blows from the north during winter. It is said to penetrate the most tightly sealed room and to have an upsetting effect on the people in its path.

▲ Modern-day Provence. The region is famous for its dramatic landscapes.

A COLOURFUL HISTORY

Following the fall of the Roman Empire, Provence was often invaded. During the Middle Ages it flourished as an independent region, with its own language, splendid courts where nobles were entertained, and great poets, known as troubadours.

Provençal literature celebrated romantic love, portraying the lover as the devoted servant of his lady. This concept spread through most of Europe and became part of the medieval idea of chivalry. As late as the 15th century, Provence was ruled independently by the celebrated 'Good Duke René'. But in 1481 the region became part of France, and over the centuries French became its official language and culture.

▲ The poet Frédéric Mistral. He wrote in Provençal in an attempt to revive the language.

PROVENÇAL REVIVAL

In the mid-19th century, an attempt was made to revive Provençal customs and to use its language for serious writing. The movement was spearheaded by a group of poets, one of whom, Frédéric Mistral (1830-1914), was later given an internationally recognized award, the Nobel Prize for Literature, for his work.

Cézanne loved the Provençal landscape and in his last years spent more and more time in the South.

A young Provençal poet, Joaquin Gasquet (1873-1921), got to know Cézanne and tried to persuade him to join the new Provençal movement. But Cézanne was clear that he was both a Provençal and part of a wider tradition – of French, and world, painting.

▲ The Pont du Gard, Provence. This Roman bridge was an aqueduct used to transport water to nearby towns.

HISTORIC PROVENCE

Ancient Greek colonists founded the first cities in Provence, including Marseilles, along the southern coast. The Romans arrived in the 2nd century BC, and in the following century the Roman leader, Julius Caesar, gave the region the name Provence, which means 'the Province' (in Latin, *Provincia*).

The Romans had a strong influence on the region. It was fertile and densely populated, and became an important centre of Roman civilisation. Today the Roman structures of Provence are world-famous. They include aqueducts (see left) and vast amphitheatres at Nîmes and Arles where gladiators once fought.

The still-life

◀ Under the Eiffel Tower, the centre-piece of the Universal Exhibition, Paris, 1889. The Exhibition was a celebration of culture, science and technology from across the globe.

REVIVING A TRADITION

In the 17th century still-lifes were especially popular among Flemish and Dutch artists, including Jan Davidsz de Heem (1606-83). In contrast to Cézanne's style, arrangements of kitchen utensils and food allowed painters to show off their skills in capturing the precise detail of the objects, their textures and reflections. The *vanitas*, a still-life with a religious message, brought together symbolic objects such as skulls and snuffed-out candles. This served to remind people that life is short.

It was not until later, in the 19th century, that the work of Manet and Cézanne gave still-life an importance it has had ever since for modern artists.

In 1888 Cézanne left Provence again and moved to Paris. Later in the year he rented a studio there.

Cézanne had always been fond of painting still-lifes. However, in *The Kitchen Table*, he applied his structural style, developed in his landscape painting, to take his still-lifes a step further.

Unlike traditional still-lifes, Cézanne's were not just copies of reality. He wanted to use a few everyday items to conjure up balanced compositions and colour harmonies. This process began before he had even picked up a brush – he propped up the objects with coins and bits of wood to make them lean in the direction he wanted.

AN INVITATION

In June 1889 Cézanne's *The House of the Hanged Man* (see page 17) was exhibited as part of the Universal Exhibition in Paris. And in November he also received an invitation to take part in an exhibition to be held the following year in Belgium. It was the first time that Cézanne's work was seen outside France.

▲ *Still-Life of Fruit*, Jan Davidsz de Heem, 1631. The detail in this painting is so precise that the food looks good enough to eat!

TIMELINE ▶

1888	December 1888	June 1889	1890
Cézanne spends five months lodging at the Hôtel Delacourt in Chantilly, outside Paris.	Cézanne moves to an apartment on the Île Saint-Louis in Paris. He rents a studio.	Opening of the Eiffel Tower in Paris. One of Cézanne's paintings is shown at the Universal Exhibition, Paris.	Three of Cézanne's works are exhibited at the Palace of Fine Arts in Brussels, Belgium. It is the first time his work is seen abroad.

The Kitchen Table, 1888-90

oil on canvas 65 x 80 cm Musée d'Orsay, Paris

This is probably Cézanne's most complex and richly painted still-life. Where necessary, he has adjusted reality to make art. Look, for example, at the table at the front: the two sections we can see of the top of it at the front (either side of the cloth) do not form a straight line!

'He made a living thing out of a tea cup.'
Wassily Kandinsky (1866-1944) talking about
Cézanne in his book On the Spiritual in Art

Robust peasants of Aix

▲ Card players outside a town café, c.1910. Cézanne painted *The Card Players* after witnessing similar scenes in Aix.

In 1890 Cézanne spent five months with Hortense and Paul in Switzerland before returning to Aix. There he lived separately from them. During this period Cézanne became interested in painting the peasants of Aix, and their solemn, solid figures appear in a series of card-playing scenes.

◄ *Self-Portrait*, c.1890, Paul Cézanne. Compare this self-portrait with that on page 19. The older Cézanne seems more confident and his style more assured.

THE FRENCH CAFÉ

The men in *The Card Players* (opposite) are sitting on either side of a small table in a café. Cafés played a special part in French social life – from the humble working man's haunt to the glittering venue on the boulevards. Except on very formal occasions people rarely entertained at home. In cafés, men (but not respectable women) could meet in a more relaxed fashion.

Cafés were famous as places where writers and artists came together to exchange ideas and form groups. Even Cézanne sometimes turned up when the Impressionists met at Parisian cafés such as the Guerbois and the Nouvelle Athènes (see page 20). Not surprisingly, many paintings of the period show café scenes.

HONOURED GUEST

Around 1890, Cézanne started experimenting with different contrasts of colour and form. People were finally beginning to recognise his talent, and in 1894 a reception was held in his honour by Monet. However, during the party, Cézanne left abruptly, not even staying to collect his paintings. Despite his growing confidence in his work, he was still suspicious of people who praised it. However, he was happy to show about 100 paintings and drawings later that year at Ambroise Vollard's gallery in Paris.

TIMELINE ▶

1890	February 1891	September 1891	1892	1894	March 1895
Cézanne spends five months in Switzerland with Hortense and Paul.	Cézanne lives in Aix, but separately from Hortense and Paul.	Cézanne moves to Paris.	Articles about Cézanne appear regularly in French magazines.	Honoured by Monet at Giverny, Cézanne leaves, believing he is being mocked.	Cézanne paints with Renoir in the countryside around Aix.

The Card Players, 1893-96
oil on canvas 47.5 x 57 cm Musée d'Orsay, Paris

Cézanne painted three pictures, of which this is the most complex and widely known, in which the players and their setting are almost identical. Only subtle details, mostly of the viewpoint, make one different from the others. This kind of series could be compared to musical 'variations on a theme'. The two men hold the cards clumsily, in hands used to outdoor work, but they are concentrating hard and taking the game very seriously.

'In the Jas de Bouffan studio there are some canvases of robust peasants ... their complexions nourished by the sun, their shoulders powerful ... they are tranquil, their sole concern is to love the earth and cultivate it.'

Joachim Gasquet, Provençal poet and Cézanne's friend

31

The man and the mountain

Cézanne had his first solo exhibition in Paris in 1895. He continued to divide his time between Paris and Aix, but the landscape of the South attracted him more and more. It was much quieter than the busy city and he enjoyed the peace and solitude of the countryside.

MONT SAINTE VICTOIRE

Cézanne painted some of the places around Aix many times, but he was almost obsessed with the Mont Sainte Victoire. This looming mountain could be seen from most places in the town, and Cézanne included it in over a hundred different oil paintings and watercolours. In the painting opposite, the view is from the quarry of Bibémus, itself one of Cézanne's favourite subjects.

▲ Mont Sainte Victoire, Aix. Although Cézanne had a studio at the Jas de Bouffan, he still worked in the countryside whenever he had the opportunity.

▲ *Mont Sainte Victoire Seen from Bellevue, c.1895.* Cézanne was interested in exploring the same subject from different viewpoints.

SERIES PAINTING

In the 19th century the series represented a new approach to painting. The Impressionist Claude Monet was the pioneer, notably in his 28 paintings of Rouen Cathedral, all shown from the same point of view. They varied only because of the different effects of the surrounding light and atmosphere.

Monet painted other series, as did Pissarro. The idea was later taken up by 20th-century artists such as Pablo Picasso (1881-1973) and Andy Warhol (1928-87). A series may seem to focus on the subject, but actually it emphasises the role of the artist in responding to a subject and selecting the elements that make each picture distinctive.

TIMELINE ▶

May 1895	November 1895	1896	1896	1897
Cézanne meets Pissarro at the exhibition of Monet's paintings of Rouen Cathedral. They are overwhelmed by what they see.	The art dealer Ambroise Vollard gives Cézanne his first one-man show in Paris.	Cézanne becomes friendly with the Provençal poet Joachim Gasquet.	Vollard sells a number of Cézanne's paintings.	A Cézanne canvas is purchased by the Berlin National Gallery.

Mont Sainte Victoire Seen from Bibémus, c.1897

oil on canvas 63.8 x 80 cm Baltimore Museum of Art, Baltimore

The vivid orange walls of the quarry rise up in the middle of the view, making a striking contrast with the cold colours of the mountain. The painting creates a powerful sense of the harsh, sun-baked landscape.

'The same subject seen from different angles offers a subject for study of the most intense interest (and so varied that I think I could occupy myself for months without changing my position).'

Paul Cézanne

Post-Impressionism

▲ *Sunday Afternoon on the Island of La Grand Jatte*, 1884-86, Georges Seurat.

In the 1860s and 1870s, the Impressionists challenged the accepted 'academic' style of painting. Once they had dared to do so, other artists appeared with even more revolutionary ideas. Cézanne learned from Impressionism but then developed his own 'more durable' art. He is often grouped with other painters who also went beyond Impressionism – in particular three younger artists who went on to pursue their own distinct styles: Georges Seurat (1859-91), Paul Gauguin (1848-1903) and Vincent van Gogh (1853-90). They were not a movement, but each made an individual contribution to the development of modern art. They have been given the loose label, Post-Impressionists.

GEORGES SEURAT

Born in 1859, Seurat became the leader of a 'Neo-Impressionist' ('New-Impressionist') school of painters while still in his twenties. His technique, known as Divisionism or Pointillism, attracted a number of followers, including an Impressionist, Pissarro.

The Impressionist landscape painters built up their pictures by putting small strokes or dabs of pure colour on to the canvas. Seurat turned the Impressionist practice into a precise system, using carefully placed dots of colour, all the same size, instead of brush-strokes; like Impressionist works, when seen from a distance they blended to create a dazzling, bright image. Seurat died when he was only 31.

PAUL GAUGUIN

Gauguin is perhaps best known for his colourful paintings of island life in the south Pacific Ocean. Though born in France in 1848, he was brought up in Peru, South America. At first a sailor, he became a businessman, painting in his spare time. In 1874 he met Pissarro at the first Impressionist Exhibition in Paris but it wasn't until 1883, at the age of 35, that he finally became a full-time artist. After bitter struggles, he spent the last years of his life on the Pacific islands of Tahiti and the Marquesas. His paintings, with their simplified forms and large areas of pure colour, have an air of mystery, especially in the many exotic scenes of native life in the Pacific.

▲ *Street Leading into Mountains,* 1891, Paul Gauguin. Gauguin painted this picture in Tahiti. Unlike van Gogh, who liked to paint things where he saw them, Gauguin preferred to paint from memory so that the image was true to what he saw in his mind rather than what was actually there.

VINCENT VAN GOGH

Most Post-Impressionists were French, but van Gogh was a Dutchman. His dramatic life has inspired books, films and even a pop song. The son of a pastor (a Protestant priest), he failed in love and in his idealistic attempts to help the poor. Finally, in the early 1880s, he became a painter and moved to France. But he remained lonely and troubled in mind, and during a breakdown he cut off part of his own ear. In 1890, still only 37, he shot himself. The thick, agitated paint surfaces and brilliant colours of van Gogh's canvases make him a pioneer of Expressionism – art that seeks to convey the artist's feelings or vision. Tragically he only became famous after his suicide in 1890.

▲ *Self-portrait,* 1889-90, Vincent van Gogh. Van Gogh painted from life but created an emotional depth through his powerful brush strokes and use of intense colour.

The art dealer

In 1898 Cézanne once again rented a studio in Paris and it was here, a year later, that he painted the *Portrait of Ambroise Vollard* (opposite).

Ambroise Vollard was a Paris art dealer, but he championed painters who were not yet appreciated, which made him an important figure. He energetically drove up the prices – and the prestige – of Cézanne's paintings.

A PAINSTAKING PROCESS

In 1899 Cézanne spent months painting Vollard's portrait. This was typical of Cézanne's way of working. He painted very slowly, building up a picture stroke by stroke. Every additional stroke or patch had to be carefully thought about and related to the colours and tones in the rest of the work.

Cézanne kept unfinished canvases in his studio for years, sometimes destroying them in a rage when they failed to satisfy him. He was utterly absorbed by his art, and in spite of his laborious methods he completed over 950 paintings during his lifetime.

▲ A detail from *Portrait of Ambroise Vollard*, 1899. Cézanne worked tirelessly to achieve the desired balance between areas of light and dark.

AMBROISE VOLLARD

Born in about 1867, Vollard started his career as a lawyer before opening a gallery, selling works of art, in Paris. He held a number of exhibitions of Cézanne's work, including one in 1895 (the artist's first one-man show), in 1898 and in 1901. He also put on the first solo shows for two of the most famous artists of the 20th century, Pablo Picasso in 1901, and Henri Matisse in 1904. Vollard commissioned many works, including a set of 100 prints by Picasso.

Vollard sat for his portrait with many painters, but his experience with Cézanne was unique. He claimed that there were no less than 115 sittings, after which the painting, though a masterpiece, was still unfinished. When the dealer suggested filling an area of bare canvas on his portrait, Cézanne told him that, if he did so, he might have to scrap everything else and start again! Vollard hastily withdrew his suggestion.

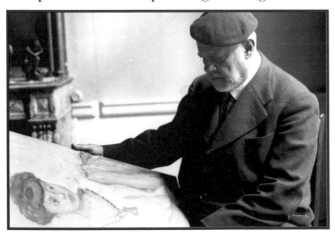

▲ Ambroise Vollard, c.1920. Through his gallery, Vollard helped establish some of the most famous names in the world.

TIMELINE ▶

October 1897	1898	1899	November 1899	1900
Cézanne's mother dies.	Cézanne rents a studio in Paris. He paints in the areas of Montgeroult and Marines.	Cézanne works in his studio on *Portrait of Ambroise Vollard*.	Cézanne sells the Jas de Bouffan. Vollard buys all the works in Cézanne's studio.	Three Cézanne paintings are shown at the Universal Exhibition, Paris.

Portrait of Ambroise Vollard, 1899
oil on canvas 92 x 65 cm Musée du Petit Palais, Paris
Vollard's portrait is a majestic work, although it was unfinished – Cézanne simply gave it
up, remarking that he was 'not displeased with the front of the shirt'! The geometrical
elements of the design influenced the 20th-century Cubist painters (see page 41).

The old master

▲ The interior of Cézanne's studio at Les Lauves. Construction of the studio was finally completed in September 1902.

CÉZANNE'S STUDIO

In 1899 Cézanne sold the Jas de Bouffan, probably because the family mansion was too big for him to run. He took an apartment in Aix-en-Provence, but he could not find a suitable studio to work in. Eventually he decided to build his own studio and in 1901 he bought a plot of land at Les Lauves, on a hillside just outside Aix. The house he built there had two storeys, the top one consisting of a single very large room with a glass wall on the north side, which flooded it with light. This became his new studio, where he worked until his death in 1906.

During his last years, Cézanne attracted a number of young admirers. Though pleased at first, he remained as eccentric and suspicious as ever, usually without good reason. In 1902 he built a studio outside Aix away from prying eyes. It was here, in 1906, that he completed *The Large Bathers* (opposite).

GRAND MASTERPIECE

The Large Bathers is the most famous example of Cézanne's bathing scenes. Many were clearly inspired by his boyhood memories of the River Arc. Here, Cézanne combines memories with sketches of the female form made while he was at the Académie Suisse, to produce a grand masterpiece that was almost 10 years in the making. Shortly after finishing it Cézanne caught pneumonia. He never recovered and died on 23 October 1906.

▲ Cézanne seated in front of a painting from his 'Large Bathers' series. In all Cézanne painted three pictures of large bathers between 1894 and 1906.

TIMELINE ▶

1901	1902	1904	1905	23 October 1906
Cézanne is honoured by Maurice Denis (1870-1943) in his painting *Homage to Cézanne*.	Death of Zola. Cézanne has a new studio, Les Lauves (now a museum).	Works by Cézanne are given an entire room at the Salon d'Automne.	Exhibition by the Fauves, led by Henri Matisse. Cézanne works at Fontainebleau, outside Paris.	Death of Cézanne.

The Large Bathers, 1906

oil on canvas 208.3 x 251.5 cm Philadelphia Museum of Art, Pennsylvania

This is one of three large-scale paintings of female bathers that Cézanne worked on during the last ten years of his life. He was determined, at any cost, to create a masterpiece in the modern figurative tradition – an equivalent to the great art of the past. To achieve his vision, he manipulated the figures of the women, lengthening an arm, or changing the angle or position of a body.

The sheer size of this version (see measurements given above) suggests that he regarded it as the grand climax to his career. It is an inspiring painting that combines Cézanne's study of the natural environment and the human form in a grand, cathedral-like composition.

'I am old, ill, and have sworn to myself to die painting.'

Paul Cézanne

39

Cézanne's legacy

During his lifetime Cézanne introduced a range of new techniques and treatments, but most of them were related to a central idea of what a picture should be. His ideas were so revolutionary that Henri Matisse declared that Cézanne was 'the father of us all'.

Cézanne treated a painting as a new creation, made by the artist and complete in itself – not a mere copy of reality. A successful painting for him was an ordered, harmonious surface, in which all the parts were equally strong. If this could only be achieved by lengthening a sitter's arm or tilting a table, Cézanne did it.

Cézanne himself remained devoted to nature as a direct source of inspiration. But the idea that the work of art was an independent creation was adopted, and taken further, by many later artists.

> ### 'Painting is what means most to me.'
>
> *Paul Cézanne*

▲ *Blue Nude III*, 1952, Henri Matisse.
This female figure has been greatly simplified by Matisse. However the influence of Cézanne's bathers remains clear. The proportions of the figure, including its long legs and thin arms, are strikingly similar to those found on page 39.

A GREAT COLOURIST

The famous French artist Henri Matisse was above all a master of colour, producing works of astonishing variety, from intricate decorations to large, simplified figures. Matisse admitted that he went back to Cézanne's work again and again for fresh ideas. This influence began at least as early as 1899, when Matisse bought a copy of Cézanne's *Three Bathers* (painted c.1879). Matisse always kept it by him, and its impact is clear in many of his works such as *Blue Nude III* (above).

Though a brilliant and revolutionary work, it would probably never have been created if Cézanne had not paved the way.

THE CUBISTS

Cézanne's concern with the basic structure of a painting had an influence on the most famous of all 20th-century artists, the Spaniard Pablo Picasso. This was especially important from 1907, when Picasso jointly led the Cubist movement in Paris with artist Georges Braque (1882-1963).

Picasso and other Cubists reduced objects to basic geometric forms, shown as though seen from many points of view at once. Though strikingly original, the Cubists' paintings were partly inspired by the underlying geometry of such works by Cézanne as *Portrait of Ambroise Vollard* (page 37). A statement made by Cézanne in a letter has been seen as a summary of Cubism: he told the young painter Emile Bernard to 'treat nature by means of the cylinder, the sphere and the cone'.

▲ *Portrait of Ambroise Vollard*, 1909, Pablo Picasso.

'I am working doggedly, for I see the Promised Land before me.'

Paul Cézanne

ENDURING INFLUENCE

Cézanne's greatness was not fully realized during his lifetime. Today, however, Cézanne has a whole room devoted to his work at the Musée d'Orsay in Paris. His studio at Les Lauves is a museum, maintained just as it was in his lifetime, displaying his painting equipment and some of his works. And the road that runs beside it has been renamed the Avenue Paul Cézanne.

◀ The Cézanne room at the Musée d'Orsay in Paris.

Letters between friends

Many letters written by Cézanne, and to him, have been lost. Fortunately a number have survived that record his long friendship with Emile Zola, which started when they were both schoolboys. The letters began in 1858, soon after Zola's poverty had forced him to leave Aix for Paris. Cézanne missed his friend greatly but Zola wrote optimistically to Cézanne, hoping that his friend would have the courage to join him.

▶ Paris, 16 April 1860, Zola to Cézanne. When Cézanne became discouraged in his efforts to paint well, Zola reminded him that work was as important as talent.

I have just finished a little picture which is, I believe, the best thing I have yet done; it represents my sister Rose reading to her doll. It is only one metre - if you like I will give it to you... But, you know, all pictures painted inside, in the studio, will never be as good as those done outside.
Goodbye, my dear friend

Paul Cézanne

There are two men inside the artist, the poet [creative person] and the worker. One is born a poet, one becomes a worker. And you, who have the spark, who possess what cannot be acquired, you complain, when all you have to do to succeed is exercise your fingers, become a worker.

Emile Zola

SUCCESS AND FAILURE

When Cézanne finally settled in Paris, he continued to see Zola, although both were now working hard. By 1866 Zola was becoming known as a journalist and art critic, but Cézanne had still had no success.

◀ Aix, about 19 October 1866, Cézanne to Zola. When Cézanne was living outside Paris, he wrote to describe his current efforts.

TIMELINE ▶

1839	1862	1868	1873	1875
1839 Paul Cézanne is born on 19 January at Aix.	**1862** At his second attempt he becomes a painter in Paris.	**May-December 1868** Cézanne spends time in Aix painting pictures of the surrounding landscape.	**1873** Cézanne spends the year in Auvers with Hortense and Paul. He works with Pissarro almost every day.	**1875** Cézanne meets Victor Chocquet, his first proper patron.
1848 Revolution in France. Louis-Napoléon Bonaparte becomes president.	**May 1863** Salon des Refusés displays work by artists, including Cézanne, whose work was rejected by the official Salon.	**1869** Cézanne meets Hortense Fiquet, who becomes his companion.	**1874** He shows three canvases at the first Impressionist Exhibition in Paris.	**1876** The second Impressionist Exhibition. Cézanne does not take part. His Salon piece is refused.
1857 Cézanne enrols in the free drawing school at Aix.	**1867** Cézanne begins to paint strange and violent scenes such as *The Murder*.	**1871** The Paris Commune is destroyed by government forces.	**Summer 1874** Cézanne spends the summer painting in Aix before moving back to Paris.	**1877** Cézanne shows 16 works at the third Impressionist Exhibition.
1861 Cézanne leaves Aix and joins the Académie Sussie in Paris. Meets Camille Pissarro.		**1872** Cézanne's son Paul is born. Cézanne works with Pissarro at Pontoise.		

TIME OF WAR

During the terrible events of the Franco-Prussian War and the Commune, Cézanne remained safely in L'Estaque, but Zola was exposed to danger before he managed to leave Paris. When it was all over, he returned to the capital.

I am now back in Batignolles [a district in Paris], like a man awakened from a bad dream. My little house is unchanged, my garden has not moved, furniture and foliage are undamaged, and I can tell myself that the two sieges [of Paris] were horrible comedies, made up to frighten children... Never have I felt so hopeful or so eager to work. Paris is coming back to life. As I've often said, our reign will soon begin.

Emile Zola

I have just received L'Oeuvre, which you were kind enough to send me. I thank the author of the Rougon-Macquart for this kind token of remembrance and ask him to allow me to press his hand in memory of old times. Ever yours under the impulse of times gone by.

Paul Cézanne

THE END OF A FRIENDSHIP

In the 1870s Zola did become very successful with his *Rougon-Macquart* series of novels. Only Cézanne's letters for this period, not Zola's, survive. Cézanne had many difficulties, and Zola often helped.

Cézanne would lament to his friend that 'I began to see nature rather late' and 'I am still striving to discover my way as a painter'. Actually he was creating masterpieces, although in his own eyes he was still far from his goal. Zola seems to have misunderstood and accepted that his friend had failed. He represented this in his novel *L'Oeuvre*, which upset Cézanne.

1878	1886	1888	1895	1902
1878 Cézanne's father discovers that his son has a family.	**1886** End of Cézanne's friendship with Zola. Cézanne marries Hortense.	**1888** Cézanne moves to an apartment on the Île Saint-Louis in Paris. He rents a studio.	**1895** Vollard gives him his first one-man show in Paris.	**1902** Death of Zola. Cézanne has a new studio, Les Lauves (now a museum).
1879-80 Cézanne spends a year at Melun.	**April 1886** Cézanne's father dies at the Jas de Bouffan. Cézanne inherits the family house and has enough money to support his family.	**1889** One of Cézanne's paintings is shown as part of the Universal Exhibition, Paris.	**1896** Vollard sells a number of Cézanne's paintings.	**1904** Works by Cézanne are given an entire room to themselves at the Salon d'Automne.
May 1881 Cézanne moves with Hortense and Paul to Pontoise where he works with Pissarro.	**1887** In Paris Cézanne is almost forgotten. Some think he must be dead.	**February 1891** Cézanne lives in Aix, but separately from Hortense and Paul.	**October 1897** Cézanne's mother dies.	**1900** His paintings are shown at the Universal Exhibition, Paris.
1882 Cézanne moves to the South of France. One of his paintings is accepted for the Salon.		**1892** Articles about Cézanne appear regularly.	**1899** Cézanne works on the portrait of Vollard.	**1906** Death of Cézanne on 23 October.
			November 1899 Cézanne sells the Jas de Bouffan.	

Glossary

atmosphere: the feeling a place has.

constructive brushwork: thick brushstrokes that remain visible and whose texture creates a pattern on the surface of the painting.

Divisionism, also called Pointillism: painting technique, developed by Georges Seurat, that uses individual dots of colour to form an entire picture.

exhibition: a public showing of art works.

Expressionism: an approach to painting which communicates an emotional state of mind rather than external reality. The Norwegian artist Edvard Munch (1863-1944), who painted *The Scream*, was a leading Expressionist.

Flemish: people from Flanders, a medieval region of north-west Europe now divided between Belgium, France and the Netherlands.

Franco-Prussian War: a war fought in 1870-71 between France and Prussia which resulted in the collapse of the Second Empire.

impasto: thickly applied paint which shows the marks of the tool it was applied with, for example, a palette knife.

Impressionists: a group of artists based in Paris during the late 19th century who painted 'impressions' of the world with broad brushstrokes of pure, unmixed colour. The group included Auguste Renoir (1841-1919), Claude Monet (1840-1926) and Edgar Degas (1834-1917).

landscape painting: a painting of natural scenery.

masterpiece: a word used to describe a great work of art.

mythology: a group of stories, surrounding a particular culture, for example, Greek mythology.

Neo-Impressionism: an art movement that developed from Impressionism which applied scientific principles to the formation of pictures. Georges Seurat was the most famous of the Neo-Impressionists.

Nobel prize: an annual global prize first given in 1901 for exceptional achievements in a particular field, including literature, medicine and peace.

palette knife: a broad knife traditionally used to load and mix colours on to a palette before painting.

Paris Commune: a revolutionary government established in Spring 1871 as a result of the French republican peace agreement with Prussia. The Commune was crushed in May 1871 by French republican forces.

patron: a wealthy individual who helps artists by financing or buying their works on a regular basis.

Pointillism: see Divisionism.

Post-Impressionists: a group of mostly French artists (although it included Dutchman Vincent van Gogh), who were inspired and influenced by the Impressionists use of pure colour. Cézanne was one of the Post-Impressionists.

Roman Empire: the areas of the world ruled by ancient Rome from around 27 BC.

Romanticism: describes a movement affecting art, literature and music between c.1780 and 1840, which went against the strict traditions of classicism and towards a more picturesque and imaginative style.

Salon: annual art exhibition organised by the French Academy. In the 19th century the jury refused works by many Impressionist and Post-Impressionist painters who then exhibited at the Salon des Refusés. The Salon des Independants was started in 1884.

self-portrait: usually a painting, showing the artist and often reflecting his or her feelings or state of mind.

socialist: a person who supports socialism, a set of political and economic beliefs that, among other things, values community equality above individual profit.

still-life: an arrangement of objects, such as flowers, food, vases or books, that an artist draws or paints.

Museums and galleries

Works by Cézanne are exhibited in museums and galleries all around the world. Some of the ones listed here are devoted solely to Cézanne, but most have a wide range of other artists' works on display.

Even if you can't visit any of these galleries yourself, you may be able to visit their websites. Gallery websites often show pictures of the artworks they have on display. Some of the websites even offer virtual tours which allow you to wander around and look at different paintings while sitting comfortably in front of your computer!

Most of the international websites detailed below include an option that allows you to view them in English.

U.S.A.

Art Institute of Chicago
111 South Michigan Avenue
Chicago, Illinois 60603-6404
www.artic.edu

Baltimore Museum of Art
10 Art Museum Drive
Baltimore MD 21218-3898
www.artbma.org

Fine Arts Museums of San Francisco
Administrative Offices
233 Post Street, 6th Floor
San Francisco, CA 94108
www.thinker.org

Museum of Fine Arts, Boston
Avenue of The Arts
465 Huntingdon Avenue
Boston
MA 02115-5523
www.mfa.org

National Gallery of Art
6th Street and Constitution Avenue, NW
Washington DC 20565
www.nga.gov

Philadelphia Museum of Art
Benjamin Franklin Parkway and 26th Street
Philadelphia, PA 19130
www.philamuseum.org/main.asp

EUROPE

Musée d'Orsay,
62 rue de Lille
75343 Paris, cedex 07
France
www.musee-orsay.fr

Musée du Louvre
75058 Paris
Cedex 01
France
www.louvre.fr

Musée du Petit Palais de la Ville de Paris
Avenue Winston-Churchill
75008 Paris
France
www.paris.org/Musees/PPalais/info.html

Národní Galerie
Staromestske námestí 12,
Prague 1
Czech Republic
www.ngprague.cz/main.php?language=en

The National Gallery
Trafalgar Square
London WC2N 5DN
England
www.nationalgallery.org.uk

National Gallery of Ireland
Merrion Square West
Dublin 2
Ireland
www.nationalgallery.ie

Neue Pinakothek
Barer Strasse 29,
D-80799
Munich, Germany
www.pinakothek.de/neue-pinakothek/

NY Carlsberg Glyptotek
Dantes Plads 7, DK - 1556
København V
Denmark
www.glyptoteket.dk

Walker Art Gallery Liverpool
William Brown Street
Liverpool
L3 8EL
England
www.nmgm.org.uk/walker

AUSTRALIA

National Gallery of Australia
Parkes Place
Canberra
ACT 2601
Australia
www.nga.gov.au

Index